CAT BREEDS

DEVON REXES

BY ABBY DOTY

WWW.APEXEDITIONS.COM

Copyright © 2025 by Apex Editions, Mendota Heights, MN 55120. All rights reserved. No part of this book may be reproduced or utilized in any form or by any means without written permission from the publisher.

Apex is distributed by North Star Editions:
sales@northstareditions.com | 888-417-0195

Produced for Apex by Red Line Editorial.

Photographs ©: Shutterstock Images, cover, 1, 4–5, 6–7, 8–9, 10–11, 12, 13, 14–15, 16–17, 18, 19, 20–21, 22–23, 26–27, 29; iStockphoto, 24

Library of Congress Control Number: 2024943035

ISBN
979-8-89250-309-9 (hardcover)
979-8-89250-347-1 (paperback)
979-8-89250-422-5 (ebook pdf)
979-8-89250-385-3 (hosted ebook)

Printed in the United States of America
Mankato, MN
012025

NOTE TO PARENTS AND EDUCATORS

Apex books are designed to build literacy skills in striving readers. Exciting, high-interest content attracts and holds readers' attention. The text is carefully leveled to allow students to achieve success quickly. Additional features, such as bolded glossary words for difficult terms, help build comprehension.

CHAPTER 1
TRICKS AND TREATS 4

CHAPTER 2
CURLY COATS 10

CHAPTER 3
COOL CATS 16

CHAPTER 4
CAT CARE 22

COMPREHENSION QUESTIONS • 28
GLOSSARY • 30
TO LEARN MORE • 31
ABOUT THE AUTHOR • 31
INDEX • 32

CHAPTER 1

TRICKS AND TREATS

A Devon rex sits on top of a desk. Her owner comes into the room. He pulls out a hoop and treats. The cat hops down and walks over to him.

Devon rexes often climb on furniture.

The cat and owner begin to practice tricks. First, the owner holds out the hoop. His cat jumps through. She gets a treat.

SMART CATS

Devon rexes are smart. Many learn how to do tricks. For example, the cats can learn to fetch. Some can even walk on tightropes. Owners can use treats to help with training.

Devon rexes have strong legs and can jump high.

After a few minutes, the owner sits down on the couch. His cat follows. She curls up nearby and takes a nap.

FAST FACT

Devon rexes are very social. The cats like to play with and be near people.

Devon rexes often follow their owners from room to room.

CHAPTER 2

CURLY COATS

In 1959, a woman in Devon County, England, found a curly-haired kitten. She named him Kirlee. She thought Kirlee was **related** to Cornish rex cats. Those cats have short, curly fur.

Devon County is in southwestern England.

The first Cornish rexes were born in the 1950s.

To create more curly-haired cats, people had Kirlee **mate** with Cornish rexes. But the kittens had straight fur. People realized Kirlee was a different type of cat.

NEW CATS

Kirlee had a **gene** that made his coat curly. But it wasn't the same gene that made Cornish rexes curly. Kirlee and his kittens were a new **breed**. He had to mate with different kinds of cats to have curly kittens.

Genes control a cat's eye color, fur pattern, and much more.

Kirlee fathered many kittens with curly hair. People called these cats Devon rexes. The breed became **popular** in many places.

FAST FACT

All Devon rexes are related to Kirlee.

14

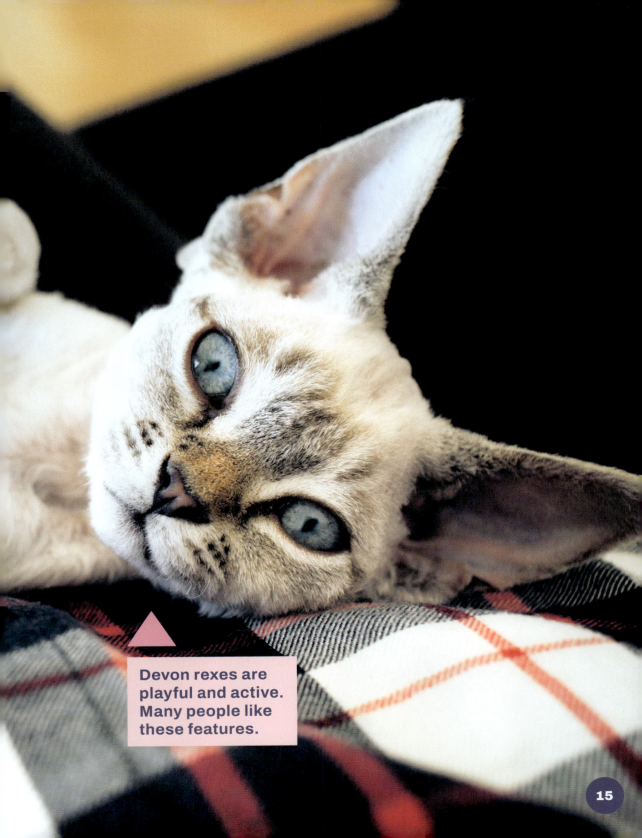

Devon rexes are playful and active. Many people like these features.

CHAPTER 3

COOL CATS

Devon rexes tend to be medium sized. The cats can weigh up to 9 pounds (4.1 kg). They have large ears and eyes. They also have long necks.

Devon rexes are known for their pointy faces.

Devon rexes have short, thin fur. The cats do not shed much. So, they can be good pets for people with **allergies**.

Devon rexes' fur comes in many different colors.

Some owners take their Devon rexes on walks.

FUR PROBLEMS
Because of their thin fur, Devon rexes may need sunscreen when they go outside. The cats can also get cold easily. They may need to wear coats.

Devon rexes are athletic cats. They like to run, climb, and **explore**. The cats also tend to be friendly and loving.

FAST FACT

Devon rexes may climb on top of doors, refrigerators, or curtain rods.

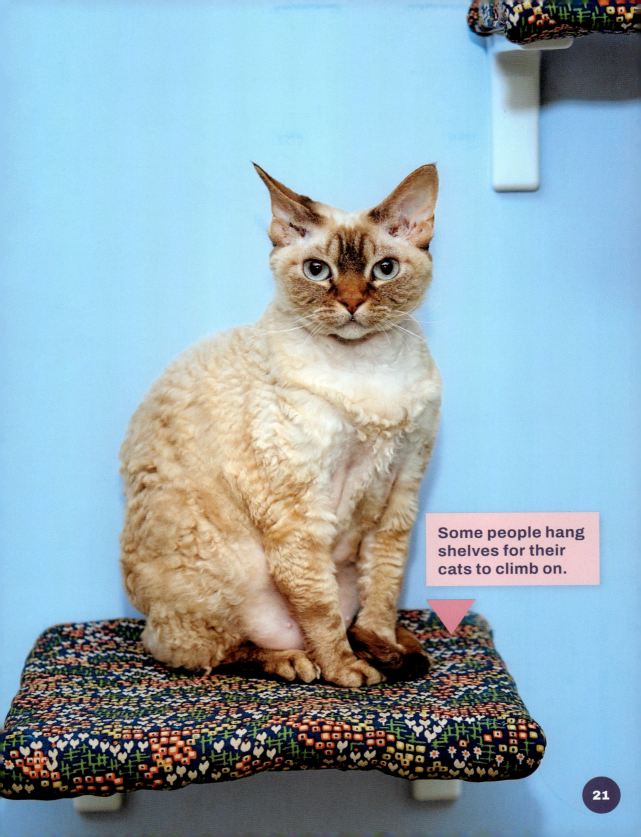

Some people hang shelves for their cats to climb on.

CHAPTER 4

CAT CARE

Devon rexes need very little brushing. In fact, too much brushing can harm their fur. Instead, owners should use damp cloths to clean the cats' fur each week.

The gene that gives Devon rexes their curly coats also makes their fur and whiskers break easily.

Devon rexes tend to get along with people and animals. The cats need lots of attention. They should not be left alone for long.

CAT PALS

Devon rexes sometimes misbehave when bored. They may scratch or damage things. So, owners may want to get two cats. That way, the cats can play with each other.

◀ Devon rexes do best with owners who can play with them every day.

FAST FACT

Devon rexes may beg for food. Owners must make sure the cats don't eat too much.

Cats should go to the vet at least once a year.

Most Devon rexes are healthy. But the breed started from **inbreeding**. So, the cats are more likely to have certain health issues. Vets can do tests to check for heart or knee problems.

COMPREHENSION QUESTIONS

Write your answers on a separate piece of paper.

1. Write a few sentences explaining the main ideas of Chapter 3.

2. Would you like to own a Devon rex? Why or why not?

3. What type of fur do Devon rexes have?
   - A. long and thin
   - B. short and thin
   - C. long and thick

4. Who or what was the Devon rex breed named after?
   - A. the people who bred Kirlee
   - B. the woman who owned Kirlee
   - C. the area where Kirlee was from

5. What does **athletic** mean in this book?

*Devon rexes are **athletic** cats. They like to run, climb, and explore.*

    A. calm and still
    B. slow and weak
    C. active and strong

6. What does **misbehave** mean in this book?

*Devon rexes sometimes **misbehave** when bored. They may scratch or damage things.*

    A. act badly
    B. act calmly
    C. act friendly

Answer key on page 32.

GLOSSARY

allergies
Reactions or responses that make people feel sick, often caused by food or animals.

breed
A specific type of cat that has its own look and abilities.

explore
To search or move through an area.

gene
A tiny part of a cell that controls how an animal looks.

inbreeding
Breeding between animals that are closely related.

mate
To come together and have babies.

popular
Liked by or known to many people.

related
Belonging to the same family.

BOOKS

Jaycox, Jaclyn. *Read All About Cats*. North Mankato, MN: Capstone Publishing, 2021.

Klukow, Mary Ellen. *Devon Rex Cats*. Mankato, MN: Amicus, 2020.

Pearson, Marie. *Cat Behavior*. Minneapolis: Abdo Publishing, 2024.

ONLINE RESOURCES

Visit **www.apexeditions.com** to find links and resources related to this title.

ABOUT THE AUTHOR

Abby Doty is a writer, editor, and booklover from Minnesota.

INDEX

A
allergies, 18

B
breed, 13
brushing, 22

C
Cornish rexes, 10, 12–13

D
Devon County, England, 10

E
ears, 16

F
fur, 10, 12, 18–19, 22

G
gene, 13

H
hoop, 4, 6

K
Kirlee, 10, 12–14
kittens, 10, 12–14

M
mate, 12–13

P
play, 8, 25

T
treats, 4, 6
tricks, 6

V
vets, 27

ANSWER KEY:
1. Answers will vary; 2. Answers will vary; 3. B; 4. C; 5. C; 6. A